Flying

Flying

prose / poems

NODIN PRESS

Grateful acknowledgment is made to the following
publications where this work first appeared, sometimes
in different versions: *Milkweed Chronicle*: "Leaf House"
and "Black Limousine"; *Lake Street Review*: "Big Deal
Baseball";*The House on Via Gombito* (New Rivers Press):
"Flying"; *Concert at Chopin's House* (New Rivers Press):
"Bread," "Forgiveness," "The Power of Dreams."

I would like to thank the McKnight Foundation and The
Loft for their generous support.

ISBN: 978-1-932472-48-6
Library of Congress Control Number: 2009909412
Book design and layout: John Toren
cover photo: DNY 59 (istock)

Nodin Press, LLC
530 N. Third Street, Suite 120
Minneapolis, MN
55401

for my sister, Barbara

Acknowledgments

My deepest gratitude to Phebe Hanson, Natalie Goldberg, Jim Moore, Cary Waterman, Paul Lisicky, Patricia Hampl, Pamela Holt, Carolyn Kleinberger, Norton Stillman, and John Toren for their help along the way. Without them, this book would not exist.

And to John, Jake, and Jennifer, my love always.

CONTENTS

One

Two

Three

~ One

LORAINE, 1942

A grey day in Grant Park,
you're sitting on a wool blanket
legs tucked under your skirt
away from the bite of the wind

blowing off Lake Michigan. The
breeze drags your hair across your
face and your eyes shine through
bright with youth and the knowledge

that the blanket will begin to float
over the lake, over the girl
children who will tether
you to them by their braids,

long brown plaits you learned
to make using the heads of your
younger sisters. Knowing the weight
of the hair, you nod your head.

The blanket begins to rise.

Leaf House

I am living in a small town in Wisconsin.

I am Polish sausage and the smell of coffee at the
Holy Name Society breakfast on Sunday morning.

I am roller skating down Marion Avenue and I see
the moon clearly and know by his features
there is a man in the moon. There is.

I am burying the baby bird that fell out of the
nest in the kitchen match box. I lead the funeral
parade around the house and we bury the pink
body in the backyard and I do not connect it with
my death, or with my father's. My father who now
reminds me of a hairless pink bird.

I am running with my sister, that good girl, that
good girl, who now has four children, four good
children, two boys and two girls, and even a dog, a
good dog, and a good husband and a good house.

I am stamping my foot the day my sister refused to
go to the movie with me to see Marilyn Monroe
and I wanted to see breasts. I wanted to see a
woman unafraid to show her sex. I wanted sex
and to have breasts and to enjoy them. I threw my
father's hairbrush in anger and it broke in two and
the act broke my anger and I knew that a girl's
anger was never any good, never did her any good.

I am selling Girl Scout cookies door to door and really think I am something going way out in the country and I am too dumb to think about how I'll have to deliver the cookies way out here.

I am twirling my baton, showing off for Barbara Marks and I knock her in the teeth and she spits them out and I realize she has false teeth although she's very young and she won't let me take the blame. I think it's the first time I've ever seen someone make a large and generous gesture because I know it was my showing off that caused it.

I am making leaf houses in the fall, "and this is the living room, and this is the kitchen, and this is the bedroom."

I am the lady of the house. I am married to somebody.

I am the lady of the leaf house.

EASTER, 1951

There we are standing in the front yard on Easter morning. My sister and I hold shiny metal pails full of jellybeans and those marshmallow chicks with beady eyes. Our mother curled our long brown hair last night by rolling it in rags before we went to bed and we tossed all night on the knots, wanting to be pretty. We wear matching coats with heavy lace collars, white hats brimming with fake daisies, violets. On our hands the white gloves, stiff and new, and too big. See how Barbara's white stockings wrinkle around her ankles; she was always thin. She wears her glasses and you can't see the right eye crossing in. She has the operation next year, when she's eight.

I remember the trips to the eye doctor, waiting in the car with our father. We talked about baseball, and how they were going to call the new team the Milwaukee Braves. I thought it had something to do with courage. I leaned over the front seat of the Chevy, looking down the shady boulevard and listened to him talk about Eddie Mathews and the Knot Hole Club. They'll cut the muscle of her eye; they'll straighten it out. She'll be sleeping and won't feel it. I imagine them taking her eye out, putting it in a white china dish next to her head, finding the muscles and reweaving them. I see them set the eye back in, blue side up, like a sapphire. She wears the white bandage a long time. When they take it off, her eye is very red, like when we both had Pinkeye, and mom leans over her at the kitchen table putting drops in, stroking her hair, telling her that everything is all right now.

We believe in the Easter bunny a long time because we want the candy. One year in the deep winter, our father misunderstands us. We see a rabbit running in the vacant lot next door. "We want it, we want the bunny," we say. He doesn't say anything but spends hours leaping after it in the snow. We lose interest and stop watching. When he returns, his face a huge smile lifted toward us with his gift, we run screaming from him. He holds the rabbit by its hind feet, blood running from its head into the white snow.

He turns from us to bury it, to bury his prize for us. If you look at the picture a little closer, you can see the snow, a small patch to the left of the sidewalk. Just one small spot left this Easter, the year we stood huddled in our spring coats, smiling for them.

Math in the Old Days

It was called arithmetic
not new or old math.
Addition, subtraction,
multiplication and
division. Long division.
We learned from
the nun in her black
habit standing
at the blackboard.
We used white chalk.
She handed me the
chalk and I stood with
my back to the class like
all the others before me
with their backs to the
class until I figured out
the answer until the bell
rang for recess and they
all went out to play but
I stood there with
my back to the class
all through recess and
all through lunch,
with my back to the class
while the geography map
rode up and down and
the Palmer's Penmanship
letters looped around the
room with my back to

the class until it was
time to go home and
the next day I came
back to the class and
did it again.

for Jake

Picnic

The food is packed in a basket, our
parents up front in the Chevrolet. Mom's hair
in a ponytail held back with a white ribbon,
red and white clip on earrings, white shorts
and a red and white halter top. Our dad welded
a metal drum into a grill before Weber made
them for America. He put charcoal briquets
and lighter fluid in the trunk next to the beer
and the cooler with the potato salad, hot dogs
and hamburgers. We spread the old army
blankets on the grass near the picnic table, away
from Marion Avenue and the heat of the
house. This day we find a good spot not too
near the family already set up at the table on
the hill. Their idea of a picnic is more elaborate
than ours, their mom is nervous and fussy
about the food. She has fried chicken and rolls
in aluminum foil, a tablecloth, and real glasses
and silverware. It takes her a long time to get
everything right. The grape kool aid in the
glasses, the chicken on a platter, the rolls and
butter on small plates. She calls her family to
the table and three children run to her to sit
in order of size opposite her at the table. Then
the dad comes, swings his legs over the seat
and sits next to her. As soon as he does, the
table flips over, the weight of both adults too
much as the three children are tossed into the
air, mouths open, chicken, rolls, kool aid and

salad everywhere. Our family runs to help, but the father leaps up angry and loud "Get away from us, we don't need your help!" We back off while he yells at his wife and kids to Goddammit! Get in the car! He takes the red and white checked tablecloth and flings all the food and plates and silverware into the center of it, opens the trunk and throws it in, shattering everything not already broken. They drive off and we see the woman looking straight ahead, the children in the back seat turned toward us, not crying, not knowing what they did wrong.

FORGIVENESS

We heard their fights. Door slam
nights to freedom at the bar for him.
Boilermakers, darts and men.

She fought on without him. Told him
off good while we sat still and fragile
as tea cups. Seen but not heard.

She always got the last word.
We turned on Ozzie & Harriet
and yearned for that bland landscape

as her heat eased out of the room.
Some time during the night the smell
of whiskey and smoke held us, rubbed

his beard against our chins and we
knew our place in the world. Forgiveness
slid from under their door and filled us

with desire: to keep the element
of fire in our eyes, to make
every day blaze alive.

Shorts

My mother made shorts for us on her Singer sewing machine. It sat in the dining room, black head hidden under walnut until she wanted it. Then, like magic, a table, a machine, a plug, and new clothes. She sewed at night after work, a red pincushion on a black elastic band worn like a corsage. She swore under her breath: shit, shit, and we went wild thinking about the new orange shorts with polka dot tops for the grade school picnic. She didn't have a buttonholer, so we wore safety pins at the waist. "Don't tuck the top in, it's supposed to be an over blouse." I studied buttonholes and tried to make one, put a slit in the shorts, but couldn't find a button big enough to keep the shorts on, so I learned how to pin from the inside. She didn't do zippers either. Everything was held together with a row of tiny snaps. We wore skirts without waistbands and hemless pants. Once she started working, sewing never saved us any money. When she decided we'd be twirlers, she made matching blue satin suits, high-necked and trimmed with pale blue sequins. As we twirled our batons, the snaps flew apart in back and there we were, her two little girls in the parade, The Spectacle of Music. She stopped sewing when the discount store opened. Atlantic Mills. You could buy a complete outfit for $7.97, never have to hem it, and we could all relax. We liked shopping at Atlantic Mills, my father outside the gang dressing room holding our coats, the three of us inside with all the others. A real women's dressing room, sagging breasts and girdles, young girls overdone in their first makeup, all trying on the lovely cheap clothes. Hanging things back on the hangers and giving free advice. "That's too tight on you, it's already ripping." and "Can you see anything through this?" I found the dress for Gloria's wedding there, all wool, and the high spike heels, the soles like cardboard, but good on a teenager with black nylons and fake pearls. We bought underwear too, packages holding seven pairs of panties, the day of the week embroidered on the front, Friday and Saturday always red and black. The smell of clothes from a store like this is unique. It's the smell of earned money, potatoes and buttermilk as a main dish, Evening in Paris perfume and Brach's chocolate covered cherries. It's the smell of plastic size tags and moving racks of men and women searching for the right thing, the covering that will keep them happy in their Chevrolet, the sky opening as they leave the parking lot with their dreams in paper bags in the trunk.

Kiss

You know how the sky turns everything hazy as it deepens into night? I remember the softness of the light and how slowly everything moved. I knew he would kiss me. I didn't know how to kiss him, so I didn't. Before it happened it felt clinical, like a science experiment. He wore a yellow knit shirt, his arms tan from playing outside. His black hair brushed back, off his forehead. And his beautiful lips. He wrapped his skinny arms around my own thin body the way kids do, hugging air. I may have touched him, but that's not what I remember. I remember the softness of his lips on my cheek. That was my last kiss in that innocent state, that state of grace granted some girls. The girls lucky enough to take their time learning love, lucky enough to meet the quiet shy boys who do not rush, who do not demand too much, who only stand with you on the creek bank under the summer night sky, open with aching and possibility. A boy took me in his arms with the potential of love and all of life did not plummet and rock. The earth stayed firm and quiet, and held that moment forever. He dropped his arms and became awkward again and we had nothing to say. I stood mute under the weight of the night and mute with storing the memory in every cell of my body. It was the last single kiss I remember with such intensity, for I have no physical emotion invested in it. No desire, no love, just gratitude for the slow path to the future.

The Truth, 1963

The truth is the wild boy asked me
   to dance and I liked him so I said
      yes. He pressed his muscled thighs

against mine and I felt his heat
   and smelled the whiskey on his breath.
      I stroked the hair on the back of his head

and he held my hand tighter and we
   swayed together in the deep colors
      moving through the room. We circled

the darkness that floated us away from
   our own small lives and when he
      asked me to go with him to his car

in the parking lot I smiled and said
   no. I turned away from him knowing
      that all I would give him was the dance

not the music inside me. We met in the dark
   gym after every game and all we did was
      dance. And that's the truth.

WHY I WEAR BLACK

My mother peers over her shoulder to see her backside in the mirror and asks, "Is this dress slimming, do I look fat?" And I am so in love with her. Remember the way your mother smells when she goes out with your father? Remember satin shoes and shiny stockings going all the way up? Remember the way your father looked at her? She absorbed our love, just as we soaked up her life, all of her. I swallowed my mother on those nights. I have kept that beautiful young woman in her black lace slip, her eyes shining as the dress slid over her head and drifted around her. She is our angel; she is the only one we see as we lie on her bed and the room tilts with her perfume. Her lips part red and she drags the tiny brush over the cake of mascara, tipping her lashes. She smoothes her eyebrows, looks at us and says, "How do I look?" and we don't see black, we don't see absence of color, we see such great and shining light, we are blinded by our lovely dressed-in-black mother.

Wedding Dance

The road turns back on itself and
I refuse to go home for the reunion.
I won't go back to the Rawson Ballroom
scene of wedding receptions and learning

to dance with the bride. A Polish beauty,
a curvy redhead before six children and
Weight Watchers, a life of green jello and
mashed potatoes. Her bridesmaids rooted

the ivy from her bouquet while she honey
mooned. A week up north in a cabin
where she rooted like an old carrot, flower
gone. Returned to the apartment above

the market, ducks flying the same way
every day on her living room wall, children
dropping like books from the shelf. Her
husband a face above her in the dark

familiar, but strange too, like her own
body, her legs turned big and blue, the
weight of her life before her. On Sunday
kneeling in the church with the promises

of Jesus melting down her throat, a great
sea of people separating her from anything
holy. At night, she hears the train taking
the town, the water tower hissing in the

field, long grass moving against her legs.
Spin around like the wedding dance. Smell
the roses in your arms, hear the man snoring
on the pillow next to you for thirty years.

The small town by the railroad tracks lives
in my bones. I visit all the time.

DIVING

The Olympics are on and I watch him walk to the edge of the platform, jump straight up and toss himself end over end, only to crack his head on the edge of the diving board. His body shoots into the water, legs folded in, no longer a person. The announcer tells us exactly how he made his mistake and a few minutes later, he mounts the platform again. I wait for him to kill himself, but he doesn't. He springs out this time and enters the water, no splash, no collapsing rag doll body. Life is full of difficult and ridiculous dives. Judges hold up numbers: one failed marriage but you remain friends, five Nines; a great second marriage, five Tens, a perfect score. No, wait. The Russian judge gives you a Nine. She knows nothing is perfect.

In 1955 my sister and I take the city bus to the swimming pool in the next town every day in the summer. Our bathing suits fade on our bodies as we climb the side entering and re-entering the blue water all afternoon. Money for the bus and a candy bar tied in the corner of a handkerchief pushed into the toe of one red sneaker. The sneakers in a wire basket with shorts and shirt, the metal safety pin with the basket number pinned to my suit, sometimes holding the strap on. We run through the cold shower before we're allowed into the white sunlight, standing in line while they check us over. Go back through the dank shower again if my suit isn't wet enough, go join the shivering snake of kids, skinny arms hugging themselves for warmth. Then the whistle between the white teeth of the lifeguard, the sound of summer starting, and the shouts of children throwing their bodies toward the water. I never really learn to swim, but stay in the shallow end, doing the dead man's float, eyes open to the moving legs below, bubbles clinging to the small hairs.

A boy grabs my legs, jerks me down, but I like him so I pretend to be afraid. Water shoots up my nose, fills me with the smell of the only ocean I know, not salt but chlorine. When I get tired, I haul myself out on my elbows, rough stone hot under my body, to fall asleep with noise all around. I put my bathing cap under my cheek and smell the rubber as the tiny mermaids etch themselves into my face.

At the end of summer, I climb the silver ladder to the high dive and stand on the end for an instant. The whole world stops as I jump off the end and the loss of control feels like a stone pulling me down, down out of a blue sky into a sea of moving children. My heart never catches up with my body, and I know I'll never jump from a high place again. It's time to go home. Find my sister, put my clothes on and everything is warm and familiar again. Stare out the window of the bus, houses flashing past, full of roast beef and mashed potatoes. I don't know yet that this is the way it will always be: back and forth with strangers, the silent acts of courage we do together, stepping off into space expecting to swim away without being hurt, to fall end over end for the rest of our lives, as if we'll always have another chance to do it over, to get it right.

ADVICE

My father came home from
welding at the factory and
changed out of his overalls,

heavy blue denim we ironed as
carefully as any dress shirt and
pants worn to church. You had to

press hard to get a sharp crease
down the front of each leg, but
nothing could hide the holes

burned through the bib, through
his blue shirt, through his white
tee shirt. When I put my finger

on the red marks scattered over
his neck like stars, he said he
didn't feel them anymore.

My mother said marry a college
graduate; my dad rubbed the
bright constellation on his chest

and said he didn't know about
college, but you can't go wrong
if you marry an electrician.

They stay clean all day.

SHARING

You know that song "Sometimes I Feel Like A Motherless Child?" Well, now it's true for me, I am one. And so is my sister. My sister, who did all the hard parts connected with our mother's death, including choosing the coffin and what she would wear, and getting the lipstick she liked over to the funeral home. Also going over to the hospital to see the body at four in the morning, so when she called with the news, inconsolable, which made me the same way, we spoke (when we could speak) about how there's no doubt that the spirit (if that's what we have) of our mother was gone. What she left was her shell, which was bathed and dressed and curled and brushed so that she almost looked like herself again. But when I touched her, as I had to, holding my sister's hand, loving that they got her hair right and the scarf draped over the folds of her neck, loving that my husband and children were there, loving my sister and her husband and their children and grandchildren, who finally relaxed and ran up to the coffin peeking in and saying goodbye to greatgrandma, then I finally felt how solid death is, how large a space it needs. I've cleared out a room in my life to contain my new guest, and since my sister and I share custody of this loss, we pass it back and forth with great tenderness, taking care to share equally, as our mother always wanted.

Up and Down

I don't know anything
for sure unless I look it up,
but sometimes I can figure
things out if I write them
down. So it's up and down
all day long. It's a good life.
Better than back and forth
or in and out which I find
constraining. I have up
and down in balance and
with my mother's death
have discovered the true
meaning of before and after.

VOICE RECOGNITION

Who knows your voice? The dog who sleeps
on your feet, who snaps his head up when you
hear nothing, who barks at the new door, who
sniffs people and turns away, nope, not that one.
Who finds the snow amazing as a white lake.

Your children. Who often refuse to respond.
That's what you get for feeding them all those
years. Now they're tall as trees and just as silent.
Maybe they'll speak to you before you die.

And your husband, if he could still hear.
So maybe only 50% of the time, when he's
wearing the hearing aids, and then there's a lot
of explaining over what he heard and what you
actually said, but still. It's fun.

And your mother, dead now, used to get your
voice confused with your sister's so you had to
identify yourself to your own mother, but she
always said Oh, I'm so glad you called, so you
spent a lot of time on the phone with her, even
when you'd covered everything twice. You
hated to say goodbye.

And your sister always knows who you are.
She even remembers who you were. She is the
one in the family who remembers everything
in its proper order, unlike you, who have a

deep pool of memories all swimming together.
You can pull a few up onto the side to spend an
hour drying off in the sun, but you always have
your sister to check the facts.

Your sister remembers how old you were when
you hopped backwards on the dock, not thinking,
always not thinking, until you hopped right off the
end into the water. Your sister pointed it out to your
father who jumped in fully clothed to bring you
back to the surface, back into the world of blue sky
and aluminum fishing boat, a large towel and the
arms of your mother.

Thanks to her, you still have a voice.

≈ Two

BLACK LIMOUSINE

Everyone travels all the time, I'm not the only one.
I travel now with a husband and it is a joy to be with him
to ride in a seat, to be cared for at the end of the trip.

Everything arranged. I am handed money in a foreign
currency, my suitcase carried by the chauffeur, the long
black car at the curb. I never rode in limousines before,

never slipped my body into the velvet blue of the backseat,
rested my head on white embroidered cloth, listened to the
clink of crystal glasses on the bar. The first time I rode

in a limousine I tried to make friends with the driver. I
wanted him to know I was a regular person; he didn't want
that. He wanted me to be someone else, a rock star,

a queen. I tried to open the back door myself, but pulled
the ashtray out of its socket instead. He said, "I'll open
the door, ma'm" as I stood there with the silver cup

in my hand. He has his job, I have mine. It's good to ride
in a long black car and let someone else drive. You forget
where you're going and where you came from. Oh, yes.

South Milwaukee, Wisconsin. Your father worked in
a factory, burned holes in his clothes with a welding torch,
drank Manhattans and played the harmonica while you

sang Red Sails in the Sunset with your mother and sister.
You ate mashed potatoes with buttermilk on Fridays and
rode the bus to your first job downtown, sat in the window

of the Electric Company and answered questions, "How much
does it cost to run the iron, and should you turn the lights off
or leave them on if you're coming right back." Cars cruised

by on Milwaukee Avenue and you waited for the bus in July
red spike heels jammed into the melted asphalt. The bus driver
knew your name, called out TGIF on Friday, your head nodding

in the first journey you took to get to work. Then the journey
was the work, was called 'taking a trip.' Leaving home in
October 1965, feeling the 727 lift off from Billy Mitchell Field

amazed at your father's tears, your father who always laughed,
never cried. Except at his brother's funeral. David who danced
and drank, committed suicide and no one ever admitted we

owned one in such despair we couldn't help. Uncle David in
our living room on Nicholson Avenue, "Serve your uncle a beer"
and somehow getting my fingers on the rim of the glass, being

told, "Don't touch the lip of the glass, don't pass germs."
No one scolds me anymore. I am not the server, I am the served.
I see, but go unseen. I ride in a black limousine.

BILLINGS, MONTANA 1966

Nineteen and away from home
for the first time. Felt how the sky
let us enter her, how she held us
from moment to moment.

I stood on the top step of the Electra
at 5 a.m. and greeted cowboys climbing
toward me in the deep freeze of January.
String ties and silver buckles, nothing

but nice guys and soldiers, before hijackers
and security, before the end of the Vietnam
war. Their long legs dangled in the aisle,
all of us in our uniforms, my red dress

high on my thigh as I reached for pillows.
And then the days we brought them home,
those boys my age, with an escort who rode
in the cabin. He pulled on his white gloves

and was the first to deplane, to meet the family
and unfold the flag on the casket. The image
most clear is the boy from Billings, Montana,
his family waiting on the tarmac. The mother

leaned into the father, the sister and brother
held everything up as if they could keep
this from coming at them. We watched from
the yellow light of the airplane as the sky

opened, as waves of rain pounded them, blurring their faces, soaking the uniform of the escort revealing his muscled body. We watched as he performed his duty slowly, with great dignity,

taking all the time in the world.

The Power of Dreams

You probably don't know this
but when you are sleeping on
an airplane the stewardess
watches you. She sees how
you curl inward, hugging
yourself, how your head lolls
back, the drool starting. She
knows how you looked as a
child. The moment the seeds
form in the corners of your
eyes, she feels you dreaming
in her body. She walks for
hours, bent over you, checking
your progress. When you all
breathe in unison, and the
aircraft hums along at the
proper pitch, she goes back
to her jump seat and closes
her eyes. You are all safe
at last, held aloft by the
power of your dreams as
you glide toward your
final destination.

Easter Sunday 1978

We are flying from Chicago to Anchorage today
on the new DC10 with forty people still strapped
in after takeoff. I am working the galley in the

tail when there is an explosion. There is nothing
like the sound of a real explosion; it happens both
inside and outside of you. I land on the floor of the

galley with meal trays falling from everywhere and all
I can think is dear God please don't let them find
me dead in the galley with lasagna and beans in my

hair. As though it mattered. The airplane goes
straight down now to make a perfect one-point
landing on it's nose and I don't know if the

captain is doing this or the airplane is now in control
of itself. The cargo doors have been blowing off
some of the DC10's and maybe that's what

happened, but we didn't decompress, and as I
jump into the aisle to check the passengers, some
are crying, some are reading the placard and

locating the nearest exit, and some are just looking at
me as if I should be doing more. The training
kicks in and we stow loose luggage and show them

how to brace for impact. Then the captain comes on
to tell us that we have flown into a flock of birds and
the explosion was the number two engine in the

tail exploding, but lucky for us it blew out not in.
We dump fuel over Lake Michigan and fly to
Duluth, which is the closest airport. The people

have to stay on board because there are no stairs
tall enough to reach the door. Now the people are coming
back to their original versions and some are angry

and some are relieved. One man gathers his
things and sits near the door. When the ground crew
builds a staircase that reaches, he departs and

says that he will never fly again. It is Easter Sunday. There
is no food available in the terminal and everyone is hungry.
I remember the lasagna, but the agent tells us we cannot

serve it; he doesn't want to be responsible for food-poisoned
people. When he deplanes, we gather in the back and decide
to call it Loaves and Fishes. I stand behind the galley table as

the passengers come past one by one, holding out the small
plastic bowls we've salvaged. I spoon lasagna and beans into
the bowls and another attendant gives them a roll and butter

smashed in gold foil. We are all happy to be here, waiting for
a new airplane to be delivered, waiting with great patience
for another chance to enter the world and rise again.

FLYING

The window is open and I hear an airplane far away. I hear the voices of all the people I served in eighteen years, a soft murmur in my life, a pool to drink from, a soothing. I remember the fire at the Hilton in Chicago, coming down nineteen flights of stairs on the outside fire escape in November. The whole thing a joke until the seventh floor and people with blackened faces, two lives gone up in smoke, two deaf boys dead in their beds. A dalmatian on the corner ran back and forth as if looking for them. The bar across the street served us coffee until only our hands shook and we remembered our names and how to walk.

Someone called their parents. Two mothers woke to hear those words while I pulled on stockings and high heels, a red uniform with my name and a half-wing on the left breast. Only half an angel, that was the joke. We flew on to Seattle and the next hotel. Always checking the back of the door now, follow the red route with my eyes: You Are Here. Still able to be located in time and space. Count the doorknobs to the exit, stay on the left, don't open the door if it feels hot, never open the window. Never, never close your eyes.

The red sun rides along the wing of the airplane, blue sky and sun always above the clouds. There is a buoyancy in the morning and the climb into the sky is effortless, silent, dreaming the way children do, without envy or greed. As if someone held our lives on strings, tangling and untangling us, the known and the unknown, glancing off each other in those sparkings between human beings. Dancing light patterns in the sky above Anchorage shoot an avalanche of memory out of the sky.

Today, an airplane breaks up on take off and the smell of a 747 rushes back. But this time I can also smell the people, the odor of fear and of plastic burning, the great intake of the last breath before the searing light. Escape of souls into the sky, still wearing seat belts, the earth unable to hold them any longer. We take off and land so many times during one lifetime. We should just stay rooted, grounded without being buried. But I flew for a while. I watched the sun rise through the cockpit window as I dipped to serve the captain his breakfast. I carried meals as if it meant something to feed thousands, patted the hands of strangers and let drunks kiss me goodbye.

And so I was with them, even though I quit flying long ago, I was with them when the airplane took off over the blue bridge of the sky, out over the water and into the deep reverie that is the long flight to Australia. I was with those nine people who were sucked through the rushing hole to death. They've given up the search; they won't find their bodies. There aren't any bodies anymore.

Imagine if two of them were your parents. They belong to you, you are made from them. Retired now, they are traveling a little and you are happy for them, and relieved. Think of your mother sitting next to the window looking for the turquoise water even though it is night. She watches the lights of Diamond Head fall away, turns, and says something to your father. He leans toward her, to listen and to see what she sees. She is always the one to point things out: Points of Interest. As a child, she was very serious, memorizing facts to please the nuns. Depth of the Pacific Ocean, names of clouds, how an aircraft stays aloft. Her hair is dyed blonde and cut short, but fluffy around her face, girlish. She wears pink lipstick and powders her nose, the only woman you know who still carries a compact.

Today she wears a blue pantsuit with a white blouse, and they both wear running shoes, although neither of them has run anywhere in a long time. She loves navy blue; her eyes are even blue. She loves the ocean, but they've always lived in the middle of the country. When she's near the ocean, she gets dreamy and seems to lose her everyday self. It's as if she could be anyone.

The terror. They must have felt it. Did she scream? Did she reach for him? Did they hold one another as they went down? Or, were they ripped apart? Were the "many small body fragments found in the crippled engine" part of them: eye, tooth, fingernail? How is any one of us safe again, flying, wondering about the fragile skin of an aging aircraft, peering into

our own mirrors at our hundreds of cracks of age.
I think about the smallest things. Where are they
floating now? If you die in an airplane engine, does
your spirit inhabit the clouds, the air around a star?
If you die in the ocean, does it wave like a small
fist around the bones of your old body?

Even if it happens very fast, I don't think it
can be fast enough not to know that you are about
to die, you are being torn apart, you are dying and
that now, surely, you are dead. I'm sure they felt
something. Cold. They felt the cold wind first,
heard the cracking, the sound of their eardrums
popping. Then I'm not sure. But maybe you die of
fright first.

The FAA is going to protect us from the
thin-skinned airplanes: there will be inspections
and grounded flights and serious looks at cargo
doors. You can't use things like we use them,
nonstop, back and forth across the ocean like that.
The aircraft should rest, too. Like a tired elephant,
it should be hosed down, fed, allowed to stay in
one place for a few days. A few nervous passengers
will joke about how we all have to go sometime.
Just don't seat me in rows eight through eleven.
Those who don't say anything will be thinking
about it on every takeoff. There are people praying
at 30,000 feet right now.

I remember another time. The DC 10
window cracked, blew out, and sucked a passenger
half out while the man behind him hung onto his
feet as the pilot aimed the plane down. Finally, the

man couldn't hold on any more and the stuck man was gone. When they interviewed him he said, "I held on, tight as I could. I really had him. Then he was just gone."

Shaking his head, the pilot said later that holding on to him through the window saved everyone else. "The man was dead when you were holding on to his feet," the pilot said, "no one could survive. The temperature at that altitude is -70 degrees." But the man who held on still believed he could have saved him, still believed that one human being can save another.

The next time you fly, feel the shape of the person sitting next to you. See the hairs on the back of the hand. Realize you both have knees. Taste the wind and roll it around in your mouth. Put your seat back before you open your book and pretend this is real. Eat whatever they place before you knowing you are just another flock of birds.

Flying is not winging over the earth alone. It is everyone breathing and believing that we'll all arrive together. In a dark place with no lights, it is someone holding you.

To Fly

What is it like to fly? I can
tell you about the way the sun
rides the wing or the way a woman
clings to me with icy hands,

a red ribbon with the word Husband
laid across the back of her seat, his
body in the belly of the aircraft.
She passed her cold fingers across

my wrist and told me how she
kissed him yesterday not knowing
it was for the last time. How she
needs coffee now, or something

don't I have something? And
when they called to tell her
this morning she was in such
a hurry, she hadn't even

washed her hair. There is
a grief so deep that all things
seem equal. This is my first
flight she said, suddenly shy.

So we rushed her to the sky.

The Word for the Day

The jump seat at door three on the DC10 faces the people.
I sit here on takeoff and landing reading the dictionary to

improve my vocabulary, to better myself. My friend Diane
made a cloth cover for my book, so the passengers assume I

am reading the Bible or a bodice ripper. I am learning two
words a day. I memorize the spelling and meaning by writing

it down and using it frequently, just like in third grade.
Today my first word is obsequious. My face flames when I

realize that I have been, at times, this word. The passengers
board and I take their garment bags to hang in the closet. One

man scowls. His bag is too heavy, even for him. I hang it in
the closet and he tells me he wants coffee before takeoff,

a pillow, a *Time* magazine would be nice, and he doesn't
know how it happened, but he really belongs in First Class.

It's okay, I say, I know how to be obsequious even back here.
He gives me a look and says, I'll bet you don't even know

what that means. Let me spell it for you, I say. Obsequious.
Submissive, docile, unassertive, deferential, tractable, mealy-

mouthed, ingratiating, bootlicking and fawning. Also brown
nosing, but I don't go that far. He laughs as though I've told

him a good joke. I don't tell him that my second word for today is obstreperous. Like the poet says: Show, don't tell.

LUCKY STAR

We walked through the old terminal in
Newark, two stewardesses in our blue
uniforms, white gloves and high heels.

In 1966 some people respected us and some
called us airheads. I was just thinking that
about the big blonde next to me when she

walked into a metal pole supporting the ceiling.
She hit it with her head and made the pole ring.
Men rushed from every corner to ask if she was

all right. She staggered on her long legs and
smiled, "Fine, thank you" to all of them. I
wondered how some of us made it from breath

to breath. I watched her through the long
afternoon and into the night as our flight
crossed the earth, never hitting anything.

Lucky star in the dark, and favored above all.

STRANGE THINGS

Strange things happen at 35,000 feet. The airplane does her slow bump and grind across the sky and I walk up and down the aisle waiting and watching. I see a man take his big hand and slam it up against the back of another man's head because he doesn't like it leaning back into his personal space. Then he puts his face in his hands and cries. The man in front of him forgives him and we fly on.

A woman boards in Chicago, an intermediate stop on our way to Seattle. She's young, nervous, a wild look in her eye. Not too many passengers today, no more than twenty in back of a 727. She changes seats three times before we take off, always sitting in the middle seat, right next to the other person, too close. We notice that she smells of last night's sex, unwashed hair, a ring of soil inside the collar of her white shirt. A brass button dangles from her navy blazer; her clothes are expensive, but she doesn't have a purse, just her ticket to ride. She won't talk to the other stewardess because Marie is blonde and she hates blondes. She follows me around, up and down the aisle, asking me where we are and do I know who she is. Some of her questions have answers, some don't.

I tell her that her job is to sit in a seat near the galley. She sits for a while, then she's up and down, sitting with the other passengers again, all of them in turn, asking them if they know who she is and how she got here. Then she tries all the empty seats, and both bathrooms. She is close to my age, twenty, but something has happened and she doesn't know where she belongs. I give her another job: to count the napkins and the swizzle sticks. She keeps asking, "Who are you?" and I say "I'm Beverly." Then she asks, "Who am I?" and I say "Look at your ticket; it has your name on it." But the name is not familiar to her and she doesn't like it.

Just before landing Marie comes into the galley and the girl jumps up, grabs the ice pick out of the ice bucket and I think we're in trouble, but she drops it and picks up the bucket, full of icy water and melting cubes, and pours it over her head, water and ice sluicing over her shoulders and onto the galley floor. "Now I know why you were looking at me funny," she says, "my hair was on fire."

When we land, the agent is there and she goes off with him. She never looks back and I never learn what happened to her. For the next two days of the trip, whenever Marie looks at me a certain way I say, "My hair is on fire, isn't it?" She nods without smiling and says, "Mine, too."

BIG DEAL BASEBALL

Everything I know
   about baseball can be
      held in one small hand.

Billy Martin.
   Eddie Mathews.
      Who's on First.

Today people fly
   from coast to coast for
      baseball. World Series.

But no one invited Japan.
   Japan would probably
      beat their socks off.

Red Sox. Black Sox. I guess the
   the United States really is the
      world and no one else matters.

Not even all those
   players the Japanese
      are so nuts about.

A World Series
   without the rest of the world.
      Big Deal Baseball. Ya Bums.

≁ Three

BREAD

The staff of life is on diets now.
It's good for you, you need it.

Whole wheat's best, but I don't
like the looks of it. It has little

chunks of stuff in it. Trees.
squirrel hairs. Coffee grounds.

It causes a strange yen for tofu
and herb tea. You begin to speak

in lettuce, broccoli is your brother.
Whole wheat bread disturbs your

brain, makes you want to read
philosophy and discontinue shaving.

You give up sugar cookies and
chocolate cake. You cry in your sleep

the pillow soft as wonder. You give
up your lover and your down comforter.

You stay home alone to bake bread,
grinding the grains with your teeth

so they are solely, wholly yours.
You grow skinny with anxiety, your blue

veins disappear, your skin grows bumps,
you become roughage. You go to the

grocery store disguised as a native, food
gathering a tribal rite, crawling down the

aisles as down the rows of living plants.
You avoid the bread aisle completely.

You cannot stand the laughter
seeping through the cellophane.

In Spite of Everything

The man rides his bike on the walking path
but he slams on the brakes when he sees the
puppy. "Hey! Is his name Sparky?" He hops

off his bike and dumps it next to me. The
puppy leaps around in joy as the man reaches
to pet him. "What d'ya think, huh, what d'ya

think, huh boy?" he says. I'm thinking this
guy could use a bath. I'm thinking a shave
and a haircut, a little deodorant. The puppy loves

the smells coming from him. He buries his nose
in the man's hands, a paradise of odor, a smell
heaven. Two white crosses dangle from silver

chains around the man's neck and the puppy tries
to mouth them. "No, no" he says, laughing, "them
are my safety." His front teeth are missing and he

reaches for a brown paper bag. "This here's
my holy water," he says, "it's not for puppies. Did
you know I got bit by a rottweiler? Right here on

my shoulder. I almost died. I got a big scar." He
pulls his shirt up and reveals the scar, raised and
purple, but the puppy sees something else and

goes after it. He watches the puppy run off and mounts his bike. "I love dogs," he says, "in spite of everything. I love you puppy!" He salutes us

and rides off into the now shimmering day.

The Black Dot

There is a black dot in the sky
above our town called hunger.
It calls in a lost voice, it wants

to go home. We begin to be
concerned. The sound it makes
careens through the streets

night after night, the same black
dot, the same cry, the same sky.
Now more of us look up, but

no one knows what to do. The
cry begins earlier each day until
we think we will go crazy, but

then we get used to it. We put
on our coats and go shopping.
We eat a good dinner and the

sound of chewing fills the space
around the cry until there is no
cry. Just the black dot in the sky.

Skating

When the lake freezes
my daughter and I
lace up our skates to
glide around, clumsy
at first, clinging to each
other, laughing. Then
the long loop around
and around, pretending
to spin, a skill we do
not actually have.
When I look at her
skate away from me,
my girl with her dark
hair flying, instead of
falling down I am
lifted up by the sight
of her leaving and
returning so fast,
so surely at her
own pace.

for Jenny

Rain

Some nights have teeth. Last
night one a.m. and something

bites you awake. The streetlight
shines under the shade or the dog

whines in her sleep. Even the pillow
won't pay attention to its work. Strange

light drips from the ceiling and you can't
figure out the message as the night slips over

into rain. Windows call to be closed and
the cold floor eats your feet as you move

through the rooms. The man beside you
breathes and you realize that your

mother sleeps alone every night now.
Carnations and satin ribbons at the funeral,

heels balanced on the edge as they lowered
your father into the dark. The headstone

holds your mother's name waiting for her
as he waited for her, always. Five years ago.

Get up and look at the calendar. Five years ago
today. The rain remembers everything now.

PROMISES

"How could you believe me when I
said I love you, when you know I've been
a liar all my life?" – Alan Jay Lerner

We were both married before and you came out
of it wanting to marry again and I came out of it
swearing never again. Which is ironic since I had
one of the most peaceful partings in the history of
divorce and am genuinely fond of my ex.

It was the idea of love, honor, and cherish for
all time that stopped me in my tracks. No more
unwitting lies for me. But you wooed me by not
promising to love me forever. Instead you chose me
every day until I believed it.

So when we stood in the living room making those
promises again, the same promises we couldn't keep
with others, we knew what we were doing. We both
knew the elusive nature of love and we took our
vows based on the solid knowledge that nothing lasts
forever.

Sooner or later, our love will die when we do, and I
promise you that I will choose you every day until I
can't.

for John

POEM FOR MY FATHER

Call me naïve, or dumb, or both
but I expected marriage to be different.

I thought my husband would become like
my father, a family man, a true companion.

Instead I spent many nights alone,
the television on, the yarn in a ball at my feet

my right hand moving in and out of the
thick thread as I tried to make something

of my life, something useful and lasting,
something that would not disintegrate. Later,

I embroidered pillowcases as my father lay
dying in the hospice trying to time my breathing

with his as he slept. The needle moved in and
out following the stamped pattern of flowers

and leaves as the real leaves swept along
the grass outside the window. The light

failed early and he told me to remember
to roll with the punches, even the ones

I don't see coming. I'd had a few poems
published and he said maybe you'll write

about me someday. And so I am writing
about him now, about how he showed

me not only how to live but how to die.
Every day without him, I roll with that.

INTO THE WORLD

They say we come into the world with nothing and we leave the same way. I agree that we leave everything behind when we die. But I believe that we arrive with everything we need.

My children were born in a far away country of different mothers. Naked they came, just like all babies, complete with their separate genetic chains allowing them to move through the world as the unique people they are, so strong and so different.

Growing up, our parents weren't much interested in our unique qualities. Don't be different, they said, try to fit in. Instructions like that actually make a child quiet and watchful. Parents would be more careful if they knew how carefully their children are watching them. Especially when you'd rather they didn't.

One little remark about someone and years later your son says, "I thought you hated her." One learns to be careful too late. It's difficult to get yourself off that particular hook and children can tell the difference between truth and lie.

Interesting that now I'm trying to determine when they might be lying to me. We taught them to look us in the eye and tell the truth. I'm afraid they also know how to look us in the eye and tell us what we

want to hear. There is nothing clear about raising
children. Nothing straightforward. There is the
fever of the tiny baby and the fever of puberty and
the fever of life passing too quickly now.

But we have made a family and we are in this
together linked by blood or love or both as we
bump from day to day bringing whatever light we
can into the world.

for Jake and Jennifer

How to Become a Stepmother

Remember: This is a test you cannot pass.
The thirteen year old asks, "Where are your kids?"
When you say you don't have any, she tells you,
"His last girlfriend did, and we are best friends."

Feel yourself slip through the blue of her eyes.
The sixteen-year-old watches you from all five
corners of the room. When her father is there
she is pleasant, smiles, asks about your cat.

When he leaves a happy man, she tries to kill you
seven different ways. She sets herself on fire
and says you did it. She watches your chest rise
and fall and hates your breath. If you try to touch

her, her arm falls off. She is a sensitive creature.
Be patient. Soon, you marry the father. The girls
come late to the wedding and pull wrinkled dresses
from paper bags to stand in the living room

crying for their mother. They throw all their arms
around the father and hold him tight within their
skirts for the last time. Stand outside yourself
in your silly white suit with the gold buttons.

Feel the orchid grieve against your cheek. Finally,
the one who hates you most reaches out and pulls
you in. Feel all their arms around you. Think,
this is my wedding. This is our wedding.

Hollywood Style

We stayed at the Bel Air hotel a few times and I always looked for movie stars. I never saw any but I did see the weddings being set up in the gazebo where a team of florists wound about a million dollars worth of flowers around the columns: orchids and lilies and lilacs and sprays of flowers at the end of each row of chairs.

As soon as one ceremony ended, a new team came in, ripped it all down, threw it away and wound different colored orchids and lilies and lilacs for the next one. The weddings had themes and for one, the groom and his groomsmen wore yellow stockings and red breeches and rode in on horses, while the bride rode in a gold carriage.

One big production after another, four in one day, a frenzy of perfection Hollywood style. It was like watching a movie being made, or like people trying out for specific roles: bride, groom, parents, friends.

I don't know who got the parts, or when it will be on the big screen or if anyone will receive an Academy Award but the swans came in from the left, as the doves flew in from the right. Next week it's elephants and airplanes.

Halloween

Here they come again, hollering
through the streets, only this year

the parents come dragging after
them, some of the dads holding

brown beer bottles. The tiny
kids trip up the steps, too scared

to make any sort of threat. The
big kids say it for them and hold

out their pillow cases and brown
bags leering in their lipstick and

hockey uniforms. There is always
one kid who grabs a handful instead

of just one or two of the little candy
bars. That's the one I love. That's

the one I wanted to be but couldn't.
The Grateful Dead sang, *Too much of*

everything is just enough. Tonight
we are not dead but we are grateful,

so I say, go ahead and take as much as
you want. Take much as you need.

Too Friendly

A woman I know who resembles my sister
walks into the restaurant, so I rise
to give her a warm embrace. She's a
little startled, but pleased to be so loved.
I see that I've been too friendly, like a
golden retriever. This has happened before.
Once I stroked a friend's cheek just
because she looked more thoughtful than
her husband. She didn't seem to mind,
but I can see that this behavior is dangerous
and you could get a certain reputation. I'm
learning to check the impulse to kiss random
people on the street, the ones who look so sad.
Instead, I pat them on the back and say:
there, there, sweetheart, you tell me your
story, and I'll tell you mine.

Dearly Departed

Some people believe that our
dearly departed try to contact us

through electrical devices. I
take a moment to run through who

might want to tell me something
from beyond. My father, especially

after a few drinks. My mother and
her mother, who loved to talk on the

phone. Who loved to talk, period.
So when the lights dim or the phone

rings and there's no one there,
I listen carefully, just in case it's for

me and I'm about to find out where
they are and what they're up to.

Dinner Party

The famous writer sits at the head of the table
after the reading, eating and talking, so relaxed the
conversation turns to a student, an especially dumb
one. There is laughter and a mocking note.

A little ping goes off in my brain because I have
been an especially dumb student, older than
everyone in the class but no wiser, full of questions,
not realizing that no one has any real answers.

The word *dumb* hangs in a bubble over my head
and I swivel toward the man sitting on my right,
who has laryngitis so it's difficult for him to speak
though his kind wife sitting across from him speaks
for him.

I turn to the man on my left, who has lost his
partner of forty years, nursing him through all the
worst parts of for better or for worse, those words
they were not allowed to speak to each other
legally, who is now nearly blind with grief.

I look across at my friend, a woman who taught
high school and college English for over fifty years,
who cannot walk now without a cane, who never
once called a student dumb.

A young woman arrives late, but sits at the far side
and cannot hear what anyone says. And there

we are at the dinner party, with *deaf* and *dumb*
and *blind* and *mute* and *lame* suspended in
the air over the white cloth. Like newborns,
we are counting on someone to be kind, to
feed us as we feel our way through the world,
occasionally touching.

for Phebe Hanson

BLACK AND WHITE

In photography class, we learn how to change the way the world looks. You hold the camera against your eye and press the shutter to let a little light in, then go into the dark to get the image out. Thirty-six tiny frames holding everything you thought you saw. I find a roll of film in a drawer and go into the darkroom to develop it, and my father's face drifts up like a ghost, months after his death. He is pale, emaciated, and I can't bring him back, no matter what I try. There are no shades of grey in this picture, only a stark black, a brilliant white. He is forever fixed in this position, far from me but always there when I need him.

FLOAT AWAY

Move your head slightly to see the river,
to watch where it bends. Like all rivers, it flows away
from you, its secrets in its belly. Raft alongside the
people you knew and feel the way they float away
as you watch. The ones you never called back, those
who changed before you did, the ones you left.

A husband watching *Jeopardy*, holding his own
hands, life without you on a couch as you break into
lightning on the other side of town. His mother, his
sisters, his brother-in-law on the land in Ohio, hand
on his green John Deere, two children in his pocket,
his wife resting her head on his shoulder in the rain.
Float away.

The small town in Wisconsin, Ardis and soup bowls
of vanilla ice cream, no front teeth, red and white
flowered house dress held together with safety pins,
playing baseball with us, knocking the ball over
Nicholson Avenue, over trucks on their way to
California, silver wheels over our dream of family.

Hike up your skirt and run the bases, past the gas
station, through the field, round up all the people
and put them back in the right order. Old priest,
love your housekeeper. Nun, wash your hands clean
with the Christmas soap. Let us learn kindness and
peace in the black of your habit. This time don't
hit the big, slow boy with the ruler so we carry the
glow of his pain under our own skin.

Hang up your clothes and read the books you were assigned, memorize the names of trees and baseball facts. Learn the shape of your star. Hear the clock ticking behind you, remember its face and always walk forward. Care about the old ones, let them go, and just let yourself float away.

Aware

It could be that I've forgotten
how to be here, that I am asleep.

The Buddhists say to stay aware,
to wake up. Every once in a while,

I do. Then I see how the sky listens
to everything. How the trees are bare

now but still there. That's what it's like,
just your bare bones with no leaves,

no birds. Only the nest resting
quietly on the highest branch.

for Natalie

About the Author

Beverly Rollwagen was born in South Milwaukee, Wisconsin, in 1945. She worked as a stewardess for eighteen years and graduated from the University of Minnesota in 1983, the same year she quit flying. Her work has been published in journals, magazines, and anthologies, and her first book, *She Just Wants*, is also from Nodin Press. Garrison Keillor has read her poems on The Writer's Almanac, she has been nominated for a Pushcart Prize, and she was the recipient of a McKnight Fellowship in Creative Prose. She lives with her husband, John, their son, Jake, and their daughter, Jennifer, in Minneapolis, Minnesota.